The Rewards of the Diligent

A Guide to Successfully Attaining Your God-Given Goals

by
Dennis Burke

The Rewards of the Diligent

*A Guide to Successfully Attaining
Your God-Given Goals*

by
Dennis Burke

Harrison House
Tulsa, Oklahoma

Unless otherwise indicated, all Scripture quotations are taken from the *King James Version* of the Bible.

8th Printing
Over 62,000 in Print

The Rewards of the Diligent
A Guide to Successfully Attaining
Your God-Given Goals
ISBN 0-89274-747-1
Revised copyright © 1995
© 1983 Dennis Burke Ministries
P. O. Box 150043
Arlington, Texas 76015

Published by Harrison House, Inc.
P. O. Box 35035
Tulsa, Oklahoma 74153

Contents

1
The Reward of Diligence

Throughout the ages, the deep, innermost desire of mankind has remained unchanged. Man wants to obtain the goals that will create within himself a lasting satisfaction and a sense of fulfillment.

When God first created man, He gave him a task, the fulfilling of which would keep him in a place of continual satisfaction and fellowship with his Creator. The task: Subdue the earth and have dominion over it (Genesis 1:28).

When Adam chose not to fulfill the task which God had given him, he severed the close, intimate relationship with God he had previously enjoyed.

The inherent desire within man, however, continued. He still wanted to achieve and attain an objective. But now there were new objectives, ones not originating from the heart of God. Since those new goals were not governed by God, they became self-centered and self-serving.

There is no lasting satisfaction in accomplishing anything outside of the activities and ideas inspired by God. The only means of accomplishing the desires and goals most important in human life is through re-establishing the relationship which God originally designed.

The person who is diligent in the kingdom of God will see with increasing clarity the goals that God has designed for him. As they become vivid, he must continue to seek God, and to live by His standard, in order to bring those goals into reality.

> **But without faith it is impossible to please him: for he that cometh to God must believe that he is, and that he is a rewarder of them that diligently seek him.**
>
> **Hebrews 11:6**

It is those who are diligent in the Word of God who receive His rewards. But we must realize that diligence is an inward thing. It cannot be measured by outward "busyness." Luke 10:38-42 makes clear this important distinction:

Now it came to pass, as they went, that he entered into a certain village: and a certain woman named Martha received him into her house.

And she had a sister called Mary, which also sat at Jesus' feet, and heard his word.

But Martha was cumbered about much serving, and came to him, and said, Lord, dost thou not care that my sister hath left me to serve alone? bid her therefore that she help me.

And Jesus answered and said unto her, Martha, Martha, thou art careful and troubled about many things:

But one thing is needful: and Mary hath chosen that good part, which shall not be taken away from her.

Here we find Martha occupied with the business of serving Jesus and His disciples. But her "busyness" had distracted her from the truly important thing—hearing what Jesus was saying.

Mary made a choice. She had determined to hear God's Word, even though there was much work to be done.

Who was the diligent one? Obviously it was Mary, because she was diligent to seek out God's Word. And Jesus commended her for it. Martha, on the other hand, allowed the demands of serving to distract her from her hunger to know God more intimately.

Diligence is an inward attitude expressed first in a deep desire for intimate relationship with God. Then it works its way out into the activity of serving others.

This kind of inward longing to know God more intimately never stops. The deeper your fellowship, the deeper your longing to know Him.

There are many people who outwardly have all the appearance of diligence, yet who are inwardly starved and stagnant in their relationship with God. Such people have not been diligent with what they have received from God. God does not bless slothfulness, but He rewards diligence.

The Unfaithful Steward

Shortly before Jesus was to be taken away and crucified, He began teaching the disciples about the responsibilities that would be placed upon them after He had ascended to the right hand of God the Father.

In the parable of the talents (Matthew 25:14-30), Jesus gave a clear illustration of His attitude toward the diligent and the slothful.

We can all clearly identify the "man" who set out on a far journey, leaving behind certain assets in the hands of his servants. The "man" is God. The servants are the disciples who would be entrusted with the man's goods. God would entrust to these disciples, as He has to you and me, the very life and nature of Himself. That nature of super-energized life that has been deposited in your spirit and mine is the "talent." The decision to entrust different amounts to each servant was determined by the "man," based upon his knowledge of the individual servant.

God gives individual assignments to us based upon His knowledge of us. He never asks anyone to do anything that cannot be realistically accomplished.

If you are trying to do something so far-out that it is beyond your capacity in God to complete, you had better re-evaluate your assignment to make certain it is really from God.

Through this teaching, God is revealing to us that He is a creator Who has not stopped creating. He has now called you and me to become co-creators with Him.

God expects that creative ability He has implanted within you and me to be invested in order to multiply it. It must not be allowed to lie dormant. It is to be invested into this world by imparting it to the lives of others.

Two of these servants used the talents given them and made a profit for their master. It must be kept in mind that the talents referred to here do not correspond to present-day usage of the term. A talent was not a personality trait or ability, but rather a sum of money. A talent of silver was worth about $1,000.

When the man handed over his property to each of these servants it was not just for safekeeping, but for them to invest in the interest of their master.

This talent specifically represents the abundant life that God has given us—His nature, ability, and supernatural power that reside within us. Yet, at the same time, it must be understood that all that a person has—his time, money, energy, skills—are also entrusted to him to use to further the kingdom of God.

The two faithful servants were diligent to take their master's goods and use them to increase his possessions. Their labors, devotion and faithfulness were equal, and they were each given the same welcome and the exact same reward. They discovered the key to abundant, successful, joyful living: "Invest what you have been given."

When you invest in the lives of others that which God has entrusted and imparted to you, then you find the source of joy.

Even what may seem to you to be the smallest share of God's "talent," when faithfully invested, never goes unnoticed by the Master.

God's goal is to further the kingdom. When you apply every resource available to you to accomplish the goal God has set before you, your diligence will result in reward.

The third servant of this parable was not commended, but rather rebuked as a wicked and slothful servant. He was labeled unproductive. Why? What mistakes did he make? Where did he err? Let's look at verses 24 and 25:

> **Then he which had received the one talent came and said, Lord, I knew**

11

thee that thou art an hard man, reaping where thou hast not sown, and gathering where thou hast not strawed:

And I was afraid, and went and hid thy talent in the earth: lo, there thou hast that is thine.

There was a total misunderstanding in the heart of this servant. He did not serve his master well, because he did not really know him. He did not love him as he should have. He did not have the right concept of him, as evidenced by his explanation for his lack of productivity. He tried to excuse himself by laying the blame on his master. He insulted the master by accusing him of being hard and of reaping where he had not sown. In reality, through his investment in them, the man had sown generously in each one of these servants. For these statements, the servant was called wicked.

Next, he hid the goods in the ground where they remained, but without increase. The servant was idle and fruitless. Therefore he was called slothful.

Ephesians 3:20-21 from the Phillips translation says, "Now to him who by his power within us is able to do infinitely more than we ever dare to ask or imagine—to him be glory in the Church and in Christ Jesus for ever and ever, amen!"

God has super-abundant power, and that power has been made available to every believer. The power of God, the power to accomplish anything, is within you. If it remains dormant and idle, it is fruitless and not producing what God intended. Diligence will stir up that productivity.

Finally, the servant said he was afraid. Afraid to invest. Afraid to take a risk. Afraid he might fail. He would not take a chance with his master's money. He would not take the responsibility of handling his master's goods. For that, he was called unproductive.

God was not afraid to take a risk. He took a risk in sending Jesus to this earth. There was the risk that, even after the price for the sins of humanity was paid, no one would receive the sacrifice by faith. There was a risk that these few men to whom God entrusted the furthering of the kingdom might not fulfill their assignment. God took a risk!

As you invest the ability God has given you into the lives of others, you risk rejection, you risk ridicule, you risk being misunderstood. Your faithful and wise investment *will* prove to be productive, however, and you *will* enter into continuous joy.

Dare to live the adventure of this abundant life which has been entrusted to you. In this book entitled *Paths to Power*, A.W. Tozer states: "God works as long as His people live daringly: He ceases when they no longer need His aid."[1] Dare to reach out to people.

Reason for Reward

There is a danger in looking at the rewards God wants us to receive. The danger is the frustration caused in those who want to achieve the results and reap the rewards of a diligent life of faith in the Word of God, but who refuse to live diligently.

There will always be those who will seek the reward and not the rewarder. But that does not change the fact that God gives rewards. And He does so because He knows how we are made. He is aware that the anticipation and expectation of a reward will motivate us to action.

[1]*Paths to Power* by A.W. Tozer (Harrisburg, Pennsylvania: Christian Publications, Inc.), p. 35.

David is a perfect example. He was a man after God's own heart. Yet in 1 Samuel 17:24-25, you will find that when David heard of the rich reward (including the hand in marriage of the king's own daughter), offered to the man who slew Goliath, he stood forth boldly and brought deliverance to Israel.

Certainly David's actions were motivated primarily by his love for God and his people, and a hatred for the offender. But he was also aware of the reward he could expect to receive as a result of those actions.

The widow in 1 Kings 17:13-16 obeyed the prophet Elijah when he instructed her to take her last bit of meal and oil, and prepare him a little cake with it. She was told that if she would obey him, she would not run out of meal or oil. In the midst of famine, such a promise was no doubt a tremendous motivation factor.

> **And it shall come to pass, if thou shalt hearken diligently unto the voice of the Lord thy God, to observe and to do all his commandments which I command thee this day, that the Lord thy God will set thee on high above all the nations of the earth:**

And all these blessings shall come on thee, if thou shalt hearken unto the voice of the Lord thy God.

Deuteronomy 28:1-2

The Reward of Diligence

Those who are diligent to do what God has said, will receive the reward for their actions. The blessings of God will come on them and overtake them. The blessings of God do not come automatically. It is the one who aggressively takes hold of God's Word, however, who obtains them.

Remember blind Bartimaeus? He was a beggar. A liability to society. He could not work or support a family. He was good for nothing but to beg alms by the wayside. Jesus passed the place where he sat, but did not stop. When Bartimaeus realized that it was Jesus who had passed, he knew he could receive something. He cried out loudly. He was aggressive, in spite of the ridicule and opposition of those who stood around him. Because of his diligence and aggressiveness, he received his sight that day. He knew what he could receive. When Jesus asked him what he wanted, he boldly proclaimed, *Lord, that I might receive my sight* (Mark 10:51).

Bartimaeus had boldness, not brazenness. He was confident that Jesus wanted him to see. He knew that God's blessing was not automatic, but that it was obtainable. The desires that God has placed within your spirit, and the goals that He has set for you in His Word, will not be fulfilled automatically. They are, however, obtainable.

There are three points to remember in order to accomplish your God-given desires and goals:

- **Build a strong foundation in your life.** Establish yourself on God's Word.

- **Allow yourself to increase one step at a time.** Romans 4:12 refers to the steps Abraham took as he followed God. Results do not always appear overnight, but they will come. If you are patient and persistent, you will see the rewards of your diligence.

- **Set your sights high.** Let your expectation and hope be developed to the fullest. Dare to expect God's best. Then give Him your best.

Notice 2 Peter 1:5 in *The Amplified Bible:* "For this very reason, adding your diligence [to the divine promises], employ every effort in exercising your faith to develop virtue (excellence, resolution, Christian energy)...."

It is important to realize that diligence and effort must be applied to the promises of God if His rewards are to become a way of life. Peter goes on to enumerate other things that must be developed: the knowledge of God, self-control, consistency in the Word of God, godliness, brotherly affection and the God kind of love.

It takes determination in the Word of God to cultivate these areas of your life. But as you do, you will experience God's mighty power at work in the different aspects of your life.

Jesus taught that the kingdom of God worked in this manner—from within. He said, *The kingdom of heaven is like unto leaven, which a woman took, and hid in three measures of meal, till the whole was leavened* (Matthew 13:33).

The laws and principles of God's kingdom continue to work in every part of your life, as long as you continue in His Word. Learn how to meditate on God's Word. It will activate ideas within you that will be inspired by God. Use the tool of speaking in tongues which God has given you. God makes available to every believer a supernatural language to enable him to pray God's perfect will from his spirit. As you meditate upon and yield yourself to God's Word, you will find yourself praying in the Spirit for yourself, and also praying God's perfect will for others. It is a precious gift from God to build you up.

Diligently attend to matters involving your money. If you will follow God's directions concerning finances, you will find the wisdom of God and the blessings of God will come upon them.

Remain in a giving attitude. God will direct you to give continually. But He will also show you how to receive. He will adjust your thinking to correspond to His thoughts.

Proverbs 13:4 says, *The soul of the sluggard desireth, and hath nothing: but the soul of the diligent shall be made fat.* God is preparing you to increase in His abundance. You cooperate with Him through your willingness to follow Him.

Then you begin to think as He does. Proverbs 21:5 says this: *The thoughts of the diligent tend only to plenteousness.* Your thoughts are seeds. The greater your thoughts become, the more seed you are planting into your life. Then those seeds of plenty produce a great harvest. That harvest is the reward of diligence.

2
Go to the Ant

One day a number of years ago, as I was fellowshiping with God, I asked Him why I wasn't experiencing certain results in my life that I knew were available to me in the Word of God. A clear answer came up in my spirit: "Like so many other people, the reason you do not experience the results you are promised is because you are lazy!"

The message was direct. There were certain aspects of basic Christian living that I had temporarily laid aside. It was nothing that most people would call major. When there is something, however, which is robbing you of the success which God paid a dear price to give you, God sees it as major.

Proverbs 6:6-8 provides some important insight into successful Christian living:

> Go to the ant, thou sluggard; consider her ways, and be wise:

> **Which having no guide, overseer, or ruler,**
>
> **Provideth her meat in the summer, and gathereth her food in the harvest.**

There is a tremendous lesson available to the Christian who will observe the ant's qualities and allow the Holy Spirit to illuminate them in his spirit.

It is with relentless zeal that the ant goes about its daily business. It is continually active and consumed with the progress of its work.

The ant is self-motivated. It requires no overseer. It is a planner which provides for itself by storing up a supply in the harvest time. The ant knows how to work together with its co-workers in harmony and singleness of purpose. It also carries its own weight and much more. As much as 50 times more than its own weight.

These are qualities that the Holy Spirit will cultivate in you if you will begin to reach out to Him.

He will become the motivator within you, moving you in the direction of achievement. He will unfold His plan to you and, by following that plan step by step, you will see things from God's vantage point.

You will not always need outside advice in order to make decisions. You will begin to develop confidence in the direction of the Holy Spirit residing within you.

Even if you seem to lack some of the positive attributes of the ant, don't let that discourage you. Become aware of the attitude God has toward you. He sees the potential of these things coming alive in you. Develop that same attitude toward yourself.

Many times it seems easier to "coast" along. But in the long run, life is what we make it to be through our decisive action. We usually accomplish just about what we set out to accomplish.

The Source of Wisdom

These spiritual qualities which are described in the ant can be attained by the person who will put forth the effort to understand God's Word. He has said, *Draw nigh to God, and he will draw nigh to you* (James 4:8).

He will help you to become the diligent person you want to be—the person who receives rewards because he is committed to the Word of God and seeks to know Him and His ways.

God is reaching out to lift you into a position of deep, consistent communion with Him. It is when you reach this stage of spiritual development that you begin to comprehend the wisdom of God in an ever-increasing depth.

The slothful person never progresses very far. He is a spiritual sluggard. He may want the right things, but he will not put out the effort necessary to meditate in the Word of God in order to find out the secrets of receiving those things. He does not understand that there are spiritual principles to receiving form God. He must meditate and seek God's wisdom, and then he will discover how to make successful decisions.

Proverbs 13:4 says, *The soul of the sluggard desireth, and hath nothing.* Desire is an important first step to receiving anything from God. It requires diligence in applying God's Word, however, to release God's creative power from your spirit and to bring that desire into reality.

One afternoon I received a call from a man who was in desperate need of a job. He wanted some guidance to know whether he should remain where he was living at that time or move to another city to seek employment. His decision had to be made within two weeks.

After discussing the matter, I directed him to set aside time each day to seek God in prayer and in the Word. He needed to have a peace within himself that his steps were being ordered of the Lord.

About 10 days later, I received another call from this man. He sounded more desperate than ever. He did not know what to do, and there were only four days left in which to make the decision. When I asked what direction he had received from God, his answer was surprising...and yet so typical. He said, "Well, I have not been able to set aside that time for prayer."

No wonder he didn't know what to do. He had made no effort to find the answer for himself. He wanted someone else to hear from God for him. He had not considered God as his source of wisdom.

Apply the Word to Increase

It is no wonder that some people never rise above their problems. They will not wholeheartedly follow God's plan for success. They will not even take the time to learn how to make the first step.

Proverbs 6:9 goes on to say this: *How long wilt thou sleep, O sluggard? when wilt thou arise out of thy sleep?* (In other words, when will you open your eyes, focus on God's answer, and begin to allow His Word to take root and govern your life for success?)

Verses 10 and 11 say: *Yet a little sleep, a little slumber, a little folding of the hands to sleep: So shall thy poverty come as one that travelleth, and thy want as an armed man.*

Notice Moffatt's translation of verse 11 on the results of slothfulness: "Yes, and poverty will pounce on you, want will overpower you." The slothful person has no power to resist poverty.

The person who is habitually lazy and averse to exertion concerning the things of God will never be able to experience a successful relationship with God, nor the fullness of His provision. If he will not make the effort to take care of everyday practical matters of life, he will not develop in spiritual areas either.

The inner qualities of the diligent person are expressed in wise business practices, financial responsibility and devotion to his work. The diligent person is dependable and will put in an honest day's work for his employer.

The slothful person, on the other hand, has little regard for the things he possesses. His house is a mess. His car is littered and dirty. He does not take the responsibility for adequately maintaining the things that he has. He looks for a way to do as little as possible.

Proverbs 12:27 in *The Amplified Bible* refers to this type of person in this way: "The slothful man will not catch his game, or roast it if he should kill it; but the diligent man will get precious possessions."

God continues to increase the person who will consider the things he receives from the Lord as precious.

I know a man who received a sizable inheritance. He lived grand for about a year. But he made no provision or plans for the future. Suddenly he came to the tragic realization that his money supply was almost depleted, and he had little to show for what he had spent. He had not gone to the ant, considered her ways, and become wise.

When you allow God's Word to govern your life, He will lead you to know how to increase. But you must be sensitive to Him to obtain and follow His wisdom.

This is an extremely important spiritual truth. You will continue to increase in the area of your life in which you are actively applying God's Word. Let the Word establish new goals for you that will enhance your ability to live an overcoming life, a life that is pleasing to God.

You have the desire to be motivated by the Word of God. Cultivate that desire. Let it begin to take root in your heart. You have the ability to be a planner because you have God's ability in you. Let the determination of the Holy Spirit make you a success at everything you put your hand to. Be established within your spirit, and He will continually draw you into a place of commitment to Him in order to bring increase into your life.

3

The Blessing
of Obedience

The only condition of man's abiding in the Garden of Eden, the one thing the creator required of him, was obedience to His command. In Genesis 2:16 it is noted, *And the Lord God commanded the man.* And in Genesis 3:11 God questions him: *Hast thou eaten of the tree, whereof I commanded thee that thou shouldest not eat?*

As long as man continued within the guidelines of God's instructions, he enjoyed a paradise. There was no misery or hard times. He was in perfect communion with God. Nothing was said of faith or love. It was obedience that determined his destiny.

Obedience always reaps the reward. Disobedience pays the penalty.

Deuteronomy 11:26-28 sums it up this way:

Behold, I set before you this day a blessing and a curse;

A blessing, if ye obey the commandments of the Lord your God...

And a curse, if you will not obey the commandments of the Lord your God...

The Price of Disobedience

Adam paid for his disobedience to God by a lifetime of toil and regret, remembering the way it used to be before his fall. The one uniting force between Adam and his seed is disobedience. The seal of union between Christ and His seed is obedience.

Romans 5:19 states, *For as by one man's disobedience many were made sinners, so by the obedience of one shall many be made righteous.* The redemption which Jesus bought consists of restoring obedience to its place.

Those who continually live contrary to the laws of God, not accepting His goodness, reap a harvest based on their rejection of God's Word.

In Exodus 4:24-26 we see where Moses was almost struck dead because of his failure to circumcise his son as God had commanded.

Thank God for a perceptive wife whose quick action saved the day.

Because of King Saul's rebellion, stubbornness and rejection of the Word of God, he lost his kingdom (see 1 Samuel 15:23). When David committed adultery, he lost the son born of disobedience (see 2 Samuel 12:13-19).

The prophet Jonah's disobedience brought him into some extreme hardships. The people of Ninevah were enemies of God's people. But because of His great love, God did not want them destroyed. He knew that the way they were living would bring them certain ruin, so He sent a prophet to deliver them from the pending disaster.

But Jonah was not so compassionate. He ran from God because he knew God had commanded him to go to Ninevah and proclaim His mercy if they would repent. Jonah didn't really want to see these people saved, so he ran away. He thought that if he refused the assignment it would mean the destruction of the city.

This type of ignorance can create terrible problems. When Jonah launched out to sea, headed as far away from Ninevah as he could go, he soon found himself faced with disaster.

The thing that separates Jonah from so many people today is his willingness to repent and accept the Word and will of God. When he was thrown into the sea, swallowed by a fish, and tied up with seaweed, Jonah did not complain to God. He did not even cry out to Him for mercy, but rather he simply laid hold upon God's promise of redemption.

> Then I said, I am cast out of thy sight; yet I will look again toward thy holy temple.
>
> The waters compressed me about, even to the soul: the depth closed me round about, the weeds were wrapped about my head.
>
> I went down to the bottoms of the mountains; the earth with her bars was about me for ever: yet hast thou brought up my life from corruption, O Lord my God.
>
> **Jonah 2:4-6**

Jonah continued to trust his life to God when all he could see around him was fish and seaweed. He knew enough about God to know that he had to look up. He looked toward God and said, "Thou brought up my life from corruption."

When you look up as Jonah did, God will get you out. Many just remain in the "belly of the fish" through continuing in the attitude of disobedience that got them there. But when Jonah began to speak the Word of the Lord, God spoke to the fish and commanded it to put him on dry ground. Jonah's eventual obedience to proclaim God's message resulted in the deliverance of 120,000 residents of Ninevah.

It is unfortunate that many times we wait until everything looks hopeless before we turn to God and ask Him to pick up the shattered pieces. We would avoid so many pitfalls if we would become more sensitive to God and in child-like faith, trust and obey the voice of our Father.

It is quite clear that disobedience is the root of misery. Through the obedience of Jesus, man has returned to his original destiny—a life of obedience. Your choice to obey God is one way in which your relationship to God and to righteousness can be maintained.

Under the guise of freedom in the Holy Spirit, many have run from the error of salvation through works, only to be caught in the deception of salvation without obedience.

The Results of Obedience

True obedience is the return to close and continual communication with God. It is as we develop the awareness of God's holy presence abiding with us that we are kept from disobeying Him. There will be an increased dependence on the Father.

The only way to do anything is to begin. Begin to commune with God and realize that His presence with you empowers you to do the things which are pleasing in His sight.

It is through this abandonment of independence that we learn to become faithful. God is looking for those who will become more dependent upon Him. When steps are made in the direction of obeying God's instructions, you put yourself in position for God's miraculous power to move in you and through you.

It was when Naaman, the great commander of the Syrian armies, came to the prophet Elisha and dipped himself the seventh time in the muddy Jordan River that he experienced the miracle he sought. He was hopelessly sick. His pride almost prevented him from going through with God's plan. But when he stepped into that river, he was saying, "I will do what the man of God has said." And the leprosy was instantly healed (see 2 Kings 5:1-14). Obedience creates an atmosphere for miracles.

In Acts 9:10-18, Ananias was told by the Lord to go and lay his hand upon Saul of Tarsus and pray for him that he might receive his sight. Ananias was simply a disciple of Jesus, but the spotlight of attention directs us to his act of obedience. He had only to obey and a wonderful miracle took place.

Do you realize that your obedience sets the stage for great things to happen? Each time you follow God's unfolding plan, you step into a new adventure in God.

Ananias was an instrument of God used to launch one of the most powerful ministries the world has ever seen.

Not everyone will be like the Apostle Paul, but there can certainly be a lot more like Ananias. Paul himself would never have experienced the great things he did had he not been obedient. He said, *I was not disobedient unto the heavenly vision* (Acts 26:19).

In the Gospel of John, we read where a man who was born blind was being questioned about how he could now see. He answered and said, *A man that is called Jesus made clay, and anointed mine eyes, and said unto me, Go to the pool of Siloam, and wash: and I went and washed, and I received sight* (John 9:11).

Did you catch his attitude? Jesus said, "GO." The blind man said, "I went and...I received." That simple act of obedience brought him his sight.

There are those who always seem to be ready with their explanation for unanswered prayer by asserting that God always answers prayer: "Sometimes He says 'yes,' and sometimes He says 'no,' and sometimes He says 'maybe later.'" What greater invention could be devised to excuse a lack of fruitfulness which actually results from disobedience to the Word of God?

Importance of the Word

One of the great secrets of obedience is to have a proper attitude toward the Word of God. We must be receptive enough to accept the Word, then committed enough to do what God tells us to do in that Word.

Today there is a tremendous amount of attention put upon our study of the Bible in order to uncover deep truths and revelation. This is certainly good. There are many, however, who are deceived by this desire to obtain new truths. In their search for knowledge, they neglect the practical influence of the Bible to make them loving, giving, fruit-producing believers.

The reason they show little evidence of the great truths they are always seeking is because they do not receive the Word of God as instruction from the Holy Spirit to be followed. To them it is simply a new idea to be discussed and put on display to impress those around them.

All newly discovered truth must become a part of your life. God is building Himself into your life through His Word, *precept upon precept; line upon line* (Isaiah 28:13). One truth must take root in order for the next to be established.

It is through sensitive listening to the Holy Spirit that the Word of God truly comes alive. Then the power of God to fulfill His Word becomes energized within you.

Allow your study of the Bible to be a thing of faith. Take it to heart and it will become the simple revelation of what God is doing for you, in you and through you.

Each time you open your Bible, expect to hear your Father speaking to you personally. Receive what He says by faith and receive the ability to yield to it, love it and continue in it.

Love Obeys

You demonstrate your love for God not by your church attendance, how much money you give, or by your teaching a Sunday school class. You demonstrate it when you are obedient to Him.

Jesus said in John 14:15, *If ye love me, keep my commandments.* You can do many good "things" with rebellion in your heart, and those "things" mean nothing.

> **He that hath my commandments, and keepeth them, he it is that loveth me: and he that loveth me shall be loved of my Father, and I will love him, and will manifest myself to him.**
> **John 14:21**

When you keep God's Word, you show your love for Him, and you receive the results of that obedience. You not only experience God's love in a deeper way, but He said He would manifest or reveal Himself to you. You can receive deeper understanding of God and His ways, but only if your heart is receptive and ready to obey. If you are to experience God's continued abundance in your life, it will require a commitment to obey His Word.

> **And this is his commandment, That we should believe on the name of his Son Jesus Christ, and love one another, as he gave us commandment.**
>
> **1 John 3:23**

God's commandment is twofold: believe on Jesus and love people. As you learn to keep God's commandments, you discover that this obedience is the key to living a life of the love of God.

First John 2:5 says, *But whoso keepeth his word, in him verily is the love of God perfected.* That love in you longs for expression. When you invest in the lives of others that which God has imparted to you, your love toward God is expressed. When you help people, you display your love to God. You will increase in God's riches—you will experience the rewards of your diligent obedience.

Obedience Pays

The fact that there are rewards does not mean they are earned. It is the attitude of the diligent, however, that opens him to the point of receiving.

God expects complete and instant obedience. This is the key to successful living. Listen to the prophet Jeremiah: "Whether it be pleasing or whether it be hard, we will obey the voice of the Lord our God to whom we are sending you, that it may be well with us when we obey the voice of the Lord our God" (Jeremiah 42:6 *Berkeley Version*).

This is unqualified commitment. A perpetual willingness. The kind of thinking that signs the bottom of the contract before anything has been filled in.

There have been many times God has instructed me to do things that did not seem easy at the time. But time after time it proved to be a seed toward something God wanted to do in my life.

Several years ago, a close friend was in a desperate financial situation. He was facing the loss of his church building. He needed thousand of dollars within a few days.

My wife and I were attending a meeting where my friend was speaking. Although he never mentioned a word about this need, God began to move on the people and several thousand dollars were given. The Holy Spirit spoke to my heart to give a thousand dollars.

Now you must understand, I had never before given a $1,000 offering. And for a good reason—I had never had a thousand dollars I could give! I had imagined the time when I would be able to give that amount. I could see myself writing out the check. Now, God was telling me that this was the time.

I turned to my wife, Vikki, and said, "I believe God wants us to give to our friend."

She agreed!

I said, "I believe He wants us to give $1,000."

Vikki looked at me and said, "So do I."

We knew we had to believe that God would do a miracle for us because we didn't have the money. But we knew that if God had instructed us to give it, He could certainly get it to us.

I acted instantly. I went to our friend after the meeting that night and committed to give him the money as God had directed. Within a few weeks we had the additional money we needed to put into that ministry.

Then I saw something clearer than I had ever seen it before: If I would commit myself to obey God's voice, He would supply me with whatever was needed to fulfill His instructions.

It was a short time later that our ministry received its first $1,000 offering by an individual. God had taken our seed that was planted in obedience and had caused it to become fruitful.

Our friend received all that he needed and did not lose the building. And we began to receive from God on a new level.

Instant obedience brings God's blessings. There is also something that I call "delayed obedience." That is when you know God has specifically told you to do something, but you wrestle with it for a time, or just plain put it off.

One time I was engaged in a meeting at a church. Toward the end of those meetings, the Holy Spirit directed me to give $200 to that ministry. But I put it off. When I got back home, I delayed in sending the money.

During the next two weeks, I noticed a sharp decrease in the ministry income. When I went before God to ask what had stopped the flow of finances, He said, "You did. I told you to send $200 to that church and you have not done it."

I immediately repented of my disobedience and made a verbal commitment to follow through with it. As soon as possible, I put a check in the mail. And the flow of finances was restored.

These are examples involving money, but of course obedience reaches far beyond that. God may direct me to go somewhere, or He may want me to call someone and encourage them or pray for them. I have learned that whatever God's commandment may be, it is to my advantage to be obedient.

Delayed obedience brings delayed results. But if I will simply do as God asks, I will continue in His rich blessings.

Obedience brings God's favor into your life. God will cause you to steadily increase.

You will not have to live under continual pressure in this life. If you are quick to do God's will, you have a deep confidence that your steps are ordered of the Lord.

4
It's How You Finish That Counts

In any race it is not the start that is remembered. It is the finish! Certainly, the better the start, the greater the possibility that the finish will be great also. It is, however, how you finish that counts.

Many of the great people of the Bible had a very good start, but their finish was a tragedy. First Corinthians 10:12 reminds us of this important possibility: *Wherefore let him that thinketh he standeth take heed lest he fall.*

This is a serious consideration. Many people begin in the Christian walk and truly start to grow and develop. Oh, they are so thrilled with their new-found faith. Their home begins to come under control. Their business takes a turn upward. Things seem to be going so well. Suddenly, the enemy puts the pressure on. It's what they do at that point that determines how they will finish.

Satan wants to destroy what God has built into you. When it looks as though you are standing well, that's when you must be on the alert for the enemy's attack. You must continue to protect the things that you have begun to enjoy in your life. You must remain strong in your spirit.

Constantly keep God's Word stirred up within you. Consider your ways. Let God's love continually grow. Don't allow yourself to take for granted that all will continue to go well. Keep your thoughts upon God's supply and your attention on His provision for you.

Examples in the Word

There are numerous people in the Bible who had a wonderful start in their endeavors with God. But though they began well, they did not have a strong finish.

Throughout the Word of God we read of people whom God has placed before us as examples. Some of these are positive examples. They serve to demonstrate that when a person follows God's plan for his life, the results will be powerful and beautiful.

There are others whose lives clearly provide a warning. The warning is this: Unless you are careful to follow God's instructions and complete your task, the destroyer is waiting to bring ruin into your life.

Look, for example, at the young prophet in 1 King 13. In obedience to God's instruction, he brought a warning to King Jeroboam of Judah. This young prophet stood before the king and proclaimed his message fearlessly. His word outraged the king who stretched out his hand and commanded that the prophet be seized. As he spoke, his hand dried up and he was unable to draw it back.

Suddenly, just as the prophet had said, God gave a sign demonstrating that the word the prophet had spoken was true. The alter which had been defiled through the king's idolatry split apart, and the ashes that were upon it spilled out.

Immediately, Jeroboam entreated the man of God to ask God to restore his hand, and it was restored. The king then wanted to become a friend to the prophet. But God had instructed him to leave the city and not to eat or drink anything there.

Quite an impressive chain of events. All because this young prophet was willing to act upon what God had spoken to him.

What a powerful beginning! But unfortunately that is not the end of the story. An old prophet was notified of the events experienced by the king. He went to find the man of God and convinced him, with a lie, to return to the city. The disobedience of the young prophet cost him his life. He was killed by a lion on the road back to Judah. A tragic finish to such a glorious beginning.

There are so many others:

- Solomon, whose godly wisdom promoted him to the place of the wealthiest king to ever live, completed the task of building a glorious temple in which to worship Jehovah. Yet, his life ended having lost that wisdom because he had given himself over to sensuality. He married women forbidden by God, and worshipped idols which he had set up in the temple of God. What a tragedy!

- Uzziah prospered as long as he sought God. He was successful as a leader of the people and his armies. But his heart was lifted up in pride and he became unfaithful to God. He died with leprosy.

- Demas was companion and co-worker with the Apostle Paul, but later betrayed Paul and went back into worldly living.

The message rings out: *Those who don't race to finish look impressive for a time, but they do not complete their race as winners.*

Be Diligent

The New American Standard Bible version of 2 Timothy 2:15 is written like this: "Be diligent to present yourself approved to God as a workman who does not need to be ashamed, handling accurately the word of truth."

This is a day-by-day effort requiring deep-rooted confidence and commitment. The Christian must constantly strive to live in a manner that is pleasing to God. He must continually walk with God.

The Christian is not one who just looks great for the 50-yard dash and then falls apart, but one who continues like a marathon runner, mile after mile.

The truly diligent person is one who digs deep and lays a solid foundation upon God's Word. Jesus said of that man, *When the flood arose, the stream beat vehemently upon that house, and could not shake it: for it was founded upon a rock* (Luke 6:48).

The deeper you dig, the sturdier your foundation becomes. Let your roots reach deep into the rock. Satan cannot move you. Bad news does shake you. Whatever "flood" the enemy tries to bring against you does not overwhelm you. You are stable and consistent because your foundation is solid.

Run With Patience

In Hebrews 12:1-3 the apostle uses a race as a powerful example of how to finish as a winner:

> Wherefore seeing we also are compassed about with so great a cloud of witnesses, let us lay aside every weight, and the sin which doth so easily beset us, and let us run with patience the race that is set before us.
>
> Looking unto Jesus the author and finisher of our faith; who for the joy

that was set before him endured the cross, despising the shame, and is set down at the right hand of the throne of God.

For consider him that endured such contradiction of sinners against himself, lest ye be wearied and faint in your minds.

Running was one of the most popular of the Olympic games at that time. The race was conducted in a stadium approximately 600 feet in length. The starting point was at the entrance, the opposite end was the goal, where the judge sat holding the prize in his hand. The eyes of each competitor were fixed on him. They could see what they were striving to win.

As we run our race, we have a great cloud of witnesses who surround us (see Hebrews 11). Each of them testify to the fact that God is faithful to His Word. These are the great people of faith who, though they may have made mistakes and experienced setbacks, found that God responded to their faith and obedience to His Word. They witness to us the fact that simple and continual action on God's Word will bring powerful results.

Looking to Jesus

If you are going to reach out for God's highest, you must look to Jesus as your source and final authority. Notice how Phillips states this challenge: "Let us run the race that we have to run with patience, our eyes fixed on Jesus the source and the goal of our faith."

Look to Jesus and not to yourself. His life-style is your goal. His life in you is your source. Recognize that it is His life in you that makes you a success at everything you do. Don't look at your lack of ability. To look continually at your own inadequacy or inability is to get your eyes off the author and finisher of your faith. He is the perfecter of your faith. As you continue to look to Him, your faith develops.

The more you see Jesus, the more you understand His ability is available to you. You begin to recognize His willingness to use His power on your behalf. His compassion is directed toward you. You can accomplish whatever God sets before you because He is your source. He is in you and His nature has been imparted to you. As you continue to look to Him and follow

Him, you are being developed. You are taking on His nature.

That is why self-consciousness is such a detriment to your Christian life. To be self-conscious means that you are more conscious of "self" than you are of God. To put self above God is actually pride. Self is part of that weight which we are to lay aside.

You must not allow self-consciousness to contain you. Reach for greater things than ever before. You have God's ability within you to insure your success.

There is also a tendency to look at the success or failure of others in determining the success or failure you can experience. You must never look to others for comparison. Second Corinthians 10:12 warns against this very thing: *For we dare not make ourselves of the number, or compare ourselves with some that commend themselves: but they measuring themselves by themselves, and comparing themselves among themselves, are not wise.*

On the contrary, you must allow the victories of others to encourage you on to victory, and the failures of others to draw you into intercession for them. You must, however, never compare yourself with someone else. Competition and comparison is a deadly trap the devil would like to use to snare believers.

I have known people whose sole motivation was to make themselves greater in the eyes of people than someone else. Unfortunately, there are ministers who have fallen into that trap. They took their eyes off Jesus and put them on men. They turned from truly uplifting people with God's Word, and became more concerned with keeping up with their contemporaries.

There is no place for competition in the Body of Christ. We are all aiming for the same goal. There is no need to keep up with the Joneses when you are looking unto Jesus.

God has a plan for every individual to fulfill. You cannot do what God has told someone else to do and be successful at it. You must look to Jesus and find out what His desire is for you, then begin to fulfill it. That will make you successful!

It is equally necessary to look to Jesus and not at your problems or the circumstances facing you.

The Apostle Peter gives the classic example of this principle. All of the disciples were in a ship and saw Jesus walking on the water. Peter wanted to walk on the water too, so he called out to Jesus and asked permission to come to Him on the water.

And he said, Come. And when Peter was come down out of the ship, he walked on the water, to go to Jesus.

But when he saw the wind boisterous, he was afraid; and beginning to sink, he cried, saying, Lord, save me.

And immediately Jesus stretched forth his hand, and caught him, and said unto him, O thou of little faith, wherefore didst thou doubt?

Matthew 14:29-31

Peter began to sink, fearing what he saw. Jesus rebuked him because of his doubt. It was Peter's doubt in the ability of Jesus that caused him to look away from Jesus. As long as Peter continued to look at Jesus, he was walking on water miraculously. As soon as he looked away, however, he sank. Once he looked back to Jesus, he continued to walk on the water until they reached the ship.

The direction in which you look will determine the direction in which you go. If you continue to look at your problems, they will seem to grow bigger and more overwhelming. When you look to Jesus, however, it becomes easy to believe that He wants to move in your life.

This does not mean to suggest that you should ignore your problems and pretend that they don't exist. Ignoring problems will never produce anything, except more problems.

When you will, with diligence, look to Jesus, He will direct you to confront the situation with His wisdom and guidance, and will direct your steps to overcome the circumstances.

As you receive Him as the source and the goal of your faith, He will direct you in applying your faith to attack the situation with the Word of God.

Look to the Word

Someone will ask, "How can I look to Jesus when I can't see Him with my eyes?" The Bible teaches that Jesus and the Word of God are one. Jesus cannot be separated from the Word, nor can the Word be separated from Jesus. Therefore when you look to the Word, you are looking to Jesus.

James 1:23-25 tells us:

> **For if any be a hearer of the word, and not a doer, he is like unto a man beholding his natural face in a glass:**
>
> **For he beholdeth himself, and goeth his way, and straightway forgetteth what manner of man he was.**
>
> **But whoso looketh into the perfect law of liberty, and continueth therein, he being not a forgetful hearer, but a doer of the work, this man shall be blessed in his deed.**

As you look into the Word of God, you not only see Jesus, you also see yourself in the light of the New Creation. That is the "natural face" that is seen in the glass. You begin to see what you are to look like as a believer. The Bible begins to paint a picture for you of the possibilities of overcoming. You begin to recognize that it is His nature in you that draws you into an overcoming life. As you continue in the "perfect law" of the New Covenant, you find His "liberty" becoming more and more of a reality.

It is the person who looks into the mirror of God's Word but does not allow it to adjust his thinking, who will fail. He looks, but he does not continue to see himself as God sees him.

You may look into the Word of God every day, but if you never act on what you are seeing, in reality, you are still going your own way. James said this man "forgetteth what manner of man he was."

When you don't see yourself completely forgiven, as God sees you, you cannot have the confidence that your prayers will be answered.

When you don't see yourself empowered with His nature and ability, you will not walk confidently into an overcoming Christian life.

As you meditate in the Word of God, you are seeing how Jesus will respond in your life. You will discover who you are in Him. You will receive revelation knowledge and understanding.

In Matthew 6:22-23 Jesus said:

The light of the body is the eye: if therefore thine eye be single, thy whole body shall be full of light.

But if thine eye be evil, thy whole body shall be full of darkness. If therefore the light that is in thee be darkness, how great is that darkness!

A single eye is one that is looking in the right direction. Having a single eye means having the right vantage point and seeing things with the right perspective. The Word of God gives you the right vantage point.

You see yourself with a new perspective: forgiven; possessing His health; at peace with God, with yourself, with people everywhere. When your spiritual sight is properly focused, when it is pure and sound, it will bring illumination into your heart.

An evil eye is one that is focused on the wrong things and is viewing things from the wrong perspective. To more clearly understand this truth, let's examine that word *evil*. It means "adversity, affliction, calamity, misery, that which causes sorrow or any other undesirable result."

To focus your attention on sin, immorality, disease, depression, poverty, or any other work of the devil, is to have an evil eye. The reason these things are evil is because they actually produce calamity and undesirable results.

But if you turn your attention to the light of God's Word, it will cause the darkness to be run out of your life. Now you will begin to consider His power in your life to be greater than the problems and temptations attacking you.

Consider Him

Hebrews 12:3 tells us, *For consider him that endured such contradiction of sinners against himself, lest ye be wearied and faint in your minds.* Notice that the writer said, "Consider Him."

Consider His example of life. He lived in total control. He was in control over sickness and disease. He was in control over demon spirits. He did not tolerate religious hypocrisy. He continually reached out to people to deliver them from the hand of the oppressor. As you look at His example, you can see the possibilities for your life.

Consider His sacrifice. When you see the completeness of what Jesus accomplished on your behalf, you will never put yourself on a low level again. You have been bought with a price. When you see the price paid, you can see your value to God. You belong to God. He has forgiven you. *You must see yourself forgiven.*

See yourself as God sees you. Not as an unworthy sinner, but as a worthy member of the Body of Christ. You are important in this family. God Himself paid an awesome price for you. You have no right to degrade what belongs to God.

Consider His resurrection. When Jesus came out of the grave, it was Satan's eternal defeat. Now you are being raised up together with Him.

Satan has been defeated in your life. Now you can live in newness of life, not governed by old habits and fears, but by the eternal Word of God. His power is in you to produce success.

As you look to Him and consider Him, you are drawing close to Him, and He will draw close and become intimate with you. *Draw nigh to God, and he will draw nigh to you* (James 4:8).

See yourself in the light of Jesus. You belong to Him. This is the key to finishing the race. Consider Jesus above all else! Look to Jesus and succeed.

5
Getting Ahead
by Looking Back

At God's command, Moses sent spies into the land of Canaan (Numbers 13). The purpose of their venture was not to see *if* the land could be taken. God had already declared, "The land belongs to you" (verse 2). They went into the land to bring back a report of the location of cities and other information needed to devise a plan for possessing what God had given them.

Upon their return, of the 12 spies sent out, only Joshua and Caleb truly believed what God had said. All of the others brought back a report of unbelief. They were not looking ahead with the proper perspective, because they failed to remember what God had done in the past. They only saw the obstacles.

Failure will always come if you quit when an obstacle stands in the way of attaining your goal. These men had allowed their minds to wander from what they knew about God. They had experienced God's deliverance, yet they hesitated to put their confidence in Him. If they had only reflected on the times when God had made them more than conquerors, they could have boldly entered into that land. Instead, they walked away, only to die in defeat outside of the Promised Land.

They missed out on God's best for their lives. Why? Because they failed to remember the God of their deliverance.

> **Yea, they turned back and tempted God, and limited the Holy One of Israel.**
>
> **They remembered not his hand, nor the day when he delivered them from the enemy.**
>
> **Psalm 78:41-42**

God had continually told His people to remember His miraculous deliverance of them from Egypt.

In explaining the purpose and significance of the Passover, Moses stated, *It is a night to be much observed unto the Lord for bringing them out from the land of Egypt* (Exodus 12:42).

Throughout the history of Israel the remembrance of God's display of power in bringing His people out of bondage has been a source of hope and strength to rekindle confidence in the God of today.

Look Back and Remember

When you look back in your own life and remember how God has provided for you in the past, you can look ahead with confidence, knowing that He will do it again.

Psalm 105 was a reminder to the children of Israel of the great works God had done for His people. Verse 5 tells us, *Remember his marvellous works that he hath done.*

In Psalm 77:11-12 the Psalmist declares:

I will remember the works of the Lord: surely I will remember thy wonders of old.

I will meditate also of all thy work, and talk of thy doings.

Look back and reflect on those things that God has accomplished in your life. Let the inspiration it creates blossom into confidence for what lies ahead.

The uncontrolled mind will always want to look back on the wrong things—the hardships and failures of the past. People who engage in such thinking allow the memory of past experiences to form an image in their minds as to what the future will hold. More of the same. They look back wishing and look forward wondering.

Your past failures don't make you a failure today. Nor do your past successes make you a success today. It is what you determine to do *now* that will decide your destiny. If you will look back and see the good things God has done in your life, you can begin to look ahead with the right perspective.

When the armies of Israel stood cowering in terror before the threat of the Philistine champion, Goliath, there was only one young man who would stand strong to meet the challenge.

David could stand boldly in the face of adversity because he could look back and see the faithfulness of God not only in the lives of the people of Israel, but in his own life as well.

In 1 Samuel 17:34-37 David said to Saul:

> Thy servant kept his father's sheep, and there came a lion, and a bear, and took a lamb out of the flock:
>
> And I went out after him, and smote him, and delivered it out of his

mouth: and when he arose against me, I caught him by his beard, and smote him, and slew him.

Thy servant slew both the lion and the bear: and this uncircumcised Philistine shall be as one of them, seeing he hath defied the armies of the living God.

David said moreover, The Lord that delivered me out of the paw of the lion, and out of the paw of the bear, he will deliver me out of the hand of this Philistine.

When David looked back and remembered God's great deliverance of him, it energized him with the confidence that this time would be no different. He saw no difference between this giant and the lion or bear. He was seeing things from God's vantage point.

David's ability to remember the marvelous works of the Lord was one of the keys to his great success as king over God's people. He could look back with the right perspective and see the possibilities for the future.

Purposely recall the works of the Lord in your life. It will prove to be a great source of strength. In Psalm 63:5-7 David wrote:

My soul shall be satisfied as with marrow and fatness; and my mouth shall praise thee with joyful lips:

When I remember thee upon my bed, and meditate on thee in the night watches.

Because thou hast been my help, therefore in the shadow of thy wings will I rejoice.

Look Ahead

Purposely forget and disregard those things of the past that bring discouragement. Paul said, "One thing I do: forgetting what lies behind and reaching forward to what lies ahead, I press on toward the goal..." (Philippians 3:13 NAS).

Satan loves to condemn you for your past failures and mistakes. But set them aside. Look ahead. When the Israelites ate that Passover meal, they ate standing, not sitting. They were looking ahead to what was before them, not at the 430 years of struggling that was behind them. They were on their feet—ready for what lay ahead.

When Jesus instituted the New Covenant, He said, *This do in remembrance of me* (Luke 22:19). Remember the price that was paid. Remember the work that was accomplished.

But also look back at what redemption has meant in your own individual life. Remember how God has moved in your situation. Then you will be ready to look forward to the new vistas which lie ahead, the possibilities, the potential, the plans God has for you.

You can see with a new perspective because you remember the marvelous works that He has done in the past.

6

Reaching for the
High Calling

The supreme quest of every true believer is to be developed by God to such a point that he becomes a more perfect tool in God's hand, one that brings pleasure to his Father.

The Christian walk is an unending journey of developing your life to the highest spiritual level. It requires decisive action, determination and discipline, as well as diligence.

In our quest, the book of Colossians encourages us:

> If ye then be risen with Christ, seek those things which are above, where Christ sitteth on the right hand of God.

> Set your affection on things above, not on things on the earth.

Colossians 3:1-2

You are risen with Christ and seated in heavenly places (Ephesians 2:6). Seek the things above. Notice the Phillips translation: "If you are then risen with Christ, reach out for the highest gifts of Heaven, where Christ reigns in power" (Colossians 3:1).

Look up! You will see the possibilities that lie ahead.

Reach for the highest gifts heaven has to offer. They are within your grasp!

Set the standard high! Seek 100 percent success. That way, even if you were to attain only one-half of what you were reaching for, you would still be ahead of the person who had set his standard at 25 percent and made it.

Set your sights as high as you can. Then allow God to show you how to attain your goal.

You can see the Apostle Paul reaching for the high calling of God for his life: "Brethren, I do not imagine that I have yet laid hold of it. But this one thing I do — forgetting everything which is past and stretching forward to what lies in front of me, with my eyes fixed on the goal I push on to secure the prize of God's heavenward call in Christ Jesus" (Philippians 3:13-14 *Weymouth*).

Paul was reaching out, pressing toward the mark, pushing toward the goal: the high calling of God.

This is not the call of his apostleship. This speaks of the call that God has for every Christian. It is a high calling. The only way to continue toward this high calling is to forget your past failures. Set aside the things Satan uses against your mind to bring you under condemnation. Your failures of the past do not make you a failure today. Your determination to succeed sets your destiny.

When you allow your past failures to dominate your thinking, you undermine any confidence you have in God's ability in your life. Don't allow those destructive, negative thoughts to remain in your mind. Thoughts of despair, ugliness, negativism, self-pity and poverty are detrimental to you. Those thoughts are seeds in your life. Those seeds will ultimately grow if you continue to nourish them.

Cultivate new thinking! Let God's Word create thoughts of prosperity, power, confidence, compassion and beauty. This is

God's nature. These new thoughts inspired by God's Word will begin to lift you into a new realm of living. They are seeds of achievement in your life. You begin to see the possibilities that have been made available through the gospel of Jesus Christ.

Now you have set the stage for your success in the kingdom of God. You have planted the seeds that will produce power in your life.

It is those who reach out to know God's ways and think His thoughts who achieve the goals God desires for them.

Psalm 103:7 says, *He made known his ways unto Moses, his acts unto the children of Israel.* The vast majority of Christians are content to see the acts of God, and those acts are exciting. But it was not enough for Moses to see God's great acts of power and deliverance. In Exodus 33:13 he sought God, saying, Shew me now thy way.

Oh, Moses saw God's powerful acts and praised Him for them. But when he sought to know God's ways, God revealed His glory to Moses as He had to no other man. The more you know God's ways, the more you can be a part of God's actions and experience God's glory.

Our High Calling

One of the things Paul prayed for the people in the church at Ephesus was: *The eyes of your understanding being enlightened; that ye may know what is the hope of his calling* (Ephesians 1:18). As Christians, each of us has that same high calling upon our life.

- **We have been called to liberty.** *For, brethren, ye have been called unto liberty* (Galatians 5:13). We have been liberated from sin, sickness, demons and fear.

- **We have been called to the fellowship of Jesus Christ.** "By Him you were called into companionship and participation with His Son, Jesus Christ our Lord" (1 Corinthians 1:9 Amplified). When God created man and placed him in the Garden of Eden, it was for a purpose. God created man for fellowship and companionship. That purpose has not been altered. Redemption was planned to restore man to the place of fellowship with God. Now that you have been made God's companion, you are an active part of what He is doing in the earth today.

- **We have been called to be conformed to the image of Jesus.** *And we know that all things work together for good to them that love God, to them who are the called according to his purpose. For whom he did foreknow, he also did predestinate to be confronted to the image of his Son, that he might be the firstborn among many brethren* (Romans 8:28-29).

The Purpose of Our Calling

As believers, we are called of God, and the primary purpose of that calling is to change us into His image. We become the reflectors of God's nature to the world.

Jesus was God in the flesh, and He perfectly revealed the desires and attitudes of the Father. You are the very flesh and bone of Jesus, the Body of Christ. He desires to so dominate you that when people are with you, they become inspired to a fresh commitment to walk with God and are uplifted by the contagious way you look at life.

People wanted to hear what Jesus had to say because He reflected His Father. They will want to listen to you because you reflect Jesus.

John G. Lake was one of the greatest men of God in this century. In his article, "Christ Liveth in Me," he states: "Christ has a purpose in you. Christ's purpose in you is to reveal Himself to you, through you and in you." He goes on to say: "God's highest is to bring out all the qualities of God in your soul, to bring out all the individuality that is in your life, not to submerge or destroy, but to change it, to energize it, to enlarge it, until all your individuality and personality and being are of the nature and substance and quality of God."

God's purpose in us is to bring our way of thinking and our attitudes into harmony with His will.

In his book, *New Creation Realities*, E.W. Kenyon writes: "As you study the Pauline Revelation you become convinced that the ultimate of every one of those epistles is the building of the Jesus life in the individual. His plan for building Himself into us is striking. We must learn to act in His stead. There must be the conscious training of our spirits to be His actual representatives."[1]

---

[1] *New Creation Realities* by E.W. Kenyon (Kenyon's Gospel Publishing Society, 1945, 1964), p. 72.

This is the goal God has set before us. We are His ambassadors here on earth to present the world with an accurate representation of our God—this God of love Who replaces man's sin's with His own righteousness, Who substitutes health and healing where there was sickness and disease, Who gives peace of mind where there has been depression, and Who forgives where there is guilt. The world has not seen that God. They have only seen God through the clouded eye of religion which never knew Him and could not possibly portray Him accurately.

We see in God's Word that the Son of God saves men from their sin, and changes their nature by His power so that they become like Him. He fills them with His Spirit, speaks through them so they would reveal Jesus, as Jesus revealed the Father.

Notice Ephesians 4:13 in Moffatt's translation:"...till we should all attain the unity of the faith and knowledge of God's Son; reaching maturity, reaching the full measure of development which belongs to the fulness of Christ."

Now notice the footnotes on this verse from A.S. Worrell's translation: "This is the highest ideal set forth in the Gospel, as that to which God would have His children aspire.

"We can scarcely imagine what this means! Can it mean less than this—that God wishes to repeat the character and life of His Son in His people? While this is an *Ideal* for all, it is approximated only by individuals, each appropriating for himself the wonderful provisions of grace in Christ Jesus."

We must reach out for maturity because only as we mature can we reflect the character of the Son of God. There is a breed of harmless Christians who lack the power of God in their life, and who represent a poor sample of the transforming power of the grace of God.

A.W. Tozer makes this pointed observation:

"We have today theological saints, who can (and must) be proved to be saints by an appeal to the Greek original. We need saints whose lives proclaim their saint-hood, and need not run to the concordance for authentication."[2]

---

[2]*Paths to Power*, A.W. Tozer, p. 10.

Our righteousness is an important legal aspect of our redemption. Far too many Christians, however, rest upon the righteousness that has been imparted by faith without allowing it to effectively produce the righteous conduct and action for which it is intended.

In the Body of Christ the world sees a reflection of Jesus. He will stand for nothing less than spotless mirrors.

We can see again from 1 Peter 2:9 that the purpose of our calling is to reveal with ever-increasing clarity the beauty of Jesus Christ. *But ye are a chosen generation, a royal priesthood, an holy nation, a peculiar people; that ye should shew forth the praises of him who hath called you out of darkness into his marvellous light.*

We are called a "holy nation." Jesus actually created a new race of people. People who belong especially to God. People with a purpose. This purpose is made clear in the Phillips translation of this verse: "It is for you now to demonstrate the goodness of him who has called you out of darkness into his amazing light."

Live Up to Your Calling!

Demonstrate His goodness! Undo the works the devil has done. Reach out into the

Spirit realm through the Word of God. It will begin to open to you a life-style of diligence. Those who demonstrate His goodness are those who are putting away the things that hold back His effectiveness.

God will create a **dream** within you, a dream of fulfilling His goals. Ascribe to that dream. Then **cultivate** a new way of thinking and speaking. Let your thoughts and words reflect the dream that is alive within you.

Then **compel** yourself to reach out and obtain God's high calling. You will become a living incarnation of His spiritual energy. This is not for the weak-hearted Christian who is looking for an effortless existence, but for the one who is ready to meet the challenge or our times with the greatness of our God.

Finally, notice 2 Timothy 2:20-21:

> **But in a great house, there are not only vessels of gold and of silver, but also of wood and of earth; and some to honour, and some to dishonour.**
>
> **If a man therefore purge himself from these, he shall be a vessel unto honour, sanctified, and meet for the master's use, and prepared unto every good work.**

Your willingness toward God is the limit of your usefulness. You have all of the right ingredients necessary to become a productive, committed believer. Discover what a life of diligence toward God can produce.

References

The Amplified Bible, New Testament. © 1954, 1958 by The Lockman Foundation, La Habra, California.

The Amplified Bible, Old Testament. © 1962, 1964 by Zondervan Publishing House, Grand Rapids, Michigan.

The Bible, A New Translation. © 1950, 1952, 1953, 1954 by James A.R. Moffatt. Harper & Row, Publishers, Inc.,New York, New York.

The Modern Language Bible, The New Berkeley Version in Modern English, Rev. Ed. © 1945, 1959, 1969, by Zondervan Publishing House, Grand Rapids, Michigan.

New American Standard Bible. © 1960, 1962, 1963, 1968, 1971, 1972, 1973, 1975, 1977 by The Lockman Foundation, La Habra, California.

The New Testament in Modern English, Rev. Ed. © 1958, 1960, 1972 by J.B. Phillips. The Macmillan Publishing Co.,Inc.,New York, New York.

New Testament in Modern Speech by Richard Francis Weymouth. © 1978 by Kregel Publications, Grand Rapids, Michigan.

The Worrell New Testament. © 1980 by A.S. Worrell. Gospel Publishing House, Springfield, Missouri.

Dennis Burke has affected thousands of people through a refreshing approach to God's Word and the power of the Holy Spirit. His ministry takes him to a different part of the United States every  week, as well as to Australia, Asia, New Zealand, Canada and the United Kingdom.

Dennis began as an associate pastor and youth minister in Southern California. There he obtained great insight into the work of the local church. In 1976, he and his wife, Vikki, moved to Fort Worth, Texas, to work with Kenneth Copeland. After two years, God led him to enter his own ministry.

Dennis is the author of several books, including *How to Meditate God's Word* and *Knowing God Intimately*. He also serves the International Convention of Faith Ministries as International Director and Trustee.

The simplicity and balance with which Dennis teaches bring powerful insight for successful Christian living.

For a complete list of tapes and books by
Dennis Burke, or to receive his publication,
Words to the Wise, write:

Dennis Burke Ministries
P.O. Box 150043
Arlington, TX 76015

*Feel free to include your prayer requests and
comments when you write.*

The Harrison House Vision

Proclaiming the truth and the power
Of the Gospel of Jesus Christ
With Excellence;

Challenging Christians to
Live victoriously,
Grow spiritually,
Know God intimately.